Science and the Bible

Also by Donald B. DeYoung

Astronomy & the Bible
Weather & the Bible
Science & the Bible, Volume 1

Science and the Bible

Volume 2

30 Scientific Demonstrations Illustrating Scriptural Truths

Donald B. DeYoung

 Baker Books

A Division of Baker Book House Co
Grand Rapids, Michigan 49516

© 1997 by Donald B. DeYoung

Published by Baker Books
a division of Baker Book House Company
P.O. Box 6287, Grand Rapids. MI 49516-6287

Third printing, May 1998

Printed in the United States of America

Library of Congress Cataloging-in-Publication Data

DeYoung, Donald B.
    Science and the Bible : 30 scientific demonstrations illustrating scriptural truths / Donald DeYoung
       p.   cm.
       1. Bible and science—Miscellanea. 2. Activity programs in Christian education. I. Title.
    BS652.D488   1994
    220.8′5—dc20   93-21085
    ISBN 0-8010-3023-4 (v.1)
    ISBN 0-8010-5773-6 (v.2)

For current information about all releases from Baker Book House, visit our web site:
                   http://www.bakerbooks.com

To **Christopher** and **Cari**
and all kids who like to
explore the creation

Contents

List of Demonstrations

1. Crystals are grown on a rock surface.
   Numbers 17:8   God makes a garden grow
2. Various liquids and solids are mixed.
   2 Kings 6:6   God has power over nature
3. Ink is added to water.
   Job 37:13   God controls the weather
4. Sticks are balanced on one's fingers.
   Psalm 16:8   Stability in a changing world
5. White light is separated into colors.
   Psalm 19:1   God's colorful artwork
6. Sound is amplified with a pin and paper.
   Psalm 139:14   The gift of hearing
7. The properties of carbon dioxide are shown.
   Proverbs 14:12   The way to heaven
8. Raisins are made to rise and fall in liquid.
   Proverbs 21:5   Seek the Lord's direction
9. Construction paper is bleached to a white color.
   Isaiah 1:18   God's complete forgiveness
10. A blind spot is demonstrated.
    Isaiah 35:5   New life in Christ
11. Floating and sinking objects are explored.
    Jeremiah 10:12   God's faithfulness
12. The cooling effect of water is measured.
    Ezekiel 34:26   The creative design of water
13. A flaming cloth does not burn.
    Daniel 3:27   God's protection
14. Boiled and fresh eggs are compared.
    Amos 3:3   Friendship with Christ
15. A stone and other objects are dissolved.
    Habakkuk 3:6   God outlasts the mountains

16. A burning candle is sealed inside a glass.
    Matthew 5:15   The gospel must be shared
17. Soda cans are compared by weight.
    Matthew 25:32   God knows our hearts
18. Creative designs are made.
    Mark 10:6   A special part of creation
19. Two plungers cannot be separated.
    Mark 10:27   God is able to save us
20. Eggshells support the weight of many books.
    Luke 12:6   God's tender care
21. A downhill race is held between objects.
    1 Corinthians 9:24   Be faithful to God
22. The colors within ink are observed.
    1 Corinthians 12:27   The church family
23. A mirror gives strange reflections.
    1 Corinthians 13:12   Understanding God's plan
24. The force of expanding seeds breaks a jar.
    2 Corinthians 5:17   Sharing the gospel
25. A radio signal is stopped.
    Ephesians 6:11   Stop Satan in his tracks
26. The surface tension of water is observed.
    Colossians 1:17   God holds the universe together
27. The apparent and actual depths of water are compared.
    Colossians 3:20   Obey your parents
28. Pepper spreads out on water.
    1 Timothy 6:11   Run from sin
29. A form of Silly Putty is made from cornstarch.
    James 1:6, 8   An unstable person
30. An object floats or sinks in water.
    James 3:4–5   The power of the tongue

Introduction

This is a second volume of Bible and science activities for kids ages 3 to 103. The book contains thirty object lessons in the form of simple experiments. Bible references are equally divided between the Old and New Testaments. Each activity has an unusual or surprising result to help catch the audience's attention and memory.

With object lessons the intended message can sometimes be obscured by the object itself. The leader should have fun with the activities, but take care to emphasize the biblical lesson before, during, and afterward. The object lesson is best kept informal, adapting the activity and application to the particular audience. The Bible lessons are kept short with this in mind.

Don't be afraid to use science object lessons with groups—a degree in rocket science is not necessary. The biblical command to subdue the earth in Genesis 1:28 includes the study and enjoyment of the details of nature. And Christians have the best of reasons for looking at the creation: We know the Creator, and can learn more about him through the study of his handiwork. The following ten hints for successful science demonstrations are repeated from the first volume.

1. Don't let demonstrations steal the show. Start with a presentation of the Scripture. Perfectly memorize it if possible. Emphasize the main point of the lesson at the conclusion so the audience will clearly remember it.

2. Practice the demonstrations ahead of time. Repetition helps bring a smooth delivery, and practice avoids surprises when you are in front of the group. Remember the five Ps: Prior practice prevents poor presentations!

3. Double-check that all needed materials are present and arranged in convenient order. Small details add up to a confident and effective presentation.

4. Adapt demonstrations and Bible lessons to your own interests and talents. Improvise with available materials; insert new ideas of local or current interest. This creativity will hold the attention of your listeners.

5. When unexpected results occur in a demonstration, laugh and build them into your presentation. The audience will understand and be on your side.

6. Read the background of the Scripture passages. If you are comfortable and familiar with the Bible story, your confidence will be apparent.

7. Good demonstrations use everyday materials. When seen again months later, these items can trigger memory of the Bible lessons. Use of common items may also encourage the audience to try the demonstrations for themselves, extending the learning process.

8. Many of the best demonstrations involve a dramatic point: an unexpected result such as a popping balloon, or something that brings "oohs" and "ahs." Good science demonstrations should be alive and exciting.

9. Have the audience participate as much as possible. Instead of the lecture approach, help the listener be a part of the Scripture lesson and demonstration.

10. Safety for you and the audience is of the highest priority in any science activity. Plan ahead for possible problems; don't take chances. Know where a first aid kit is located. If the demonstration involves a flame, have a fire extinguisher nearby.

1

The Crystal Garden

Theme: God makes a garden grow.

Bible Verse: *The next day Moses entered the Tent of the Testimony and saw that Aaron's staff, which represented the house of Levi, had not only sprouted but had budded, blossomed and produced almonds* (Num. 17:8).

Materials Needed:
Pieces of brick or charcoal briquets
Glass bowl or dish
Small container
Laundry bluing
Salt
Household ammonia
Food coloring

Bible Lesson

The Old Testament Israelites went through many cycles of rebellion against God, followed by repentance and restoration. Numbers 16 describes the rebellion of Korah and 250 of his followers. They attempted to declare themselves priests, a privilege reserved for Aaron's family. In judgment they all were

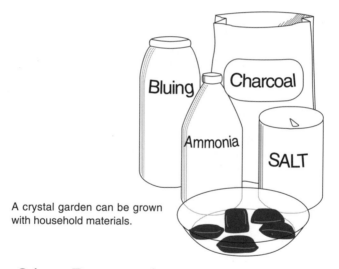

swallowed up by an earthquake. To make absolutely clear the special place of the Aaronites, God led Moses to give an object lesson. A wooden staff or walking stick from each of the twelve tribes of Israel, with the tribe's name inscribed, was placed in the Tent of Testimony. When inspected the next day, the only staff that looked different was Aaron's rod. It had supernaturally sprouted leaves and produced fruit. Here was a real example of "Miracle Grow"! The lesson was clear that Aaron's family was chosen by God to minister to the Israelites.

It is God who causes every plant to grow on the earth; he is the source of all life. At God's command, even a dead staff produces leaves and almonds. The one who controls the laws of nature is able to alter these laws at will, just as he did for Moses. God is all-powerful.

A crystal garden can be grown
with household materials.

Science Demonstration

This project takes several days to perform. In a small container mix 4 tablespoons (T) of bluing, 4 T of water, 2 T of salt, and 1 T of ammonia. Avoid breathing this mixture! Pour the solution over fragments of charcoal or brick in the bowl. Also put drops of food coloring on various parts of the charcoal, then leave the bowl undisturbed for several days.

Crystals will slowly grow like coral on the hard surfaces over 2–3 days. They are typically white, and the food coloring will give them variety. The crystals are very fragile; notice their intricate, feathery structure. The crystals will eventually collapse and fragments will begin growing throughout the bowl.

Science Explanation

The brick or charcoal provides a surface on which crystallization can occur. Capillary action causes the solution to soak upward through the fragments. Then, as the water evaporates, the chemical portion of the solution is left behind, forming the flowerlike crystals of solid salt. The rate of growth depends on the temperature and humidity of the room. Low humidity will speed the process.

Crystal growth involves much unseen activity on the submicroscopic level. To produce visible crystals in 2–3 days, hundreds of salt molecules must move through the charcoal and arrange themselves into the crystal lattice *every second*. The budding staff described in our Bible story is even more complex than crystal growth. Crystals are not alive, and certainly cannot produce almonds overnight! The growth of Aaron's staff was a miraculous sign from God.

2

The Floating Axhead

Theme: God has power over nature.

Bible Verse: *[Elisha] asked, "Where did it fall?" When he showed him the place, Elisha cut a stick and threw it there, and made the iron float* (2 Kings 6:6).

Materials Needed:
   Clear, tall glass jar or bud vase
   One-half cup each
      Dark Karo syrup or molasses (brown)
      Dishwashing liquid (blue or green)
      Vegetable oil (yellow)
      Rubbing alcohol (clear)
      Water
   Several small objects
      Cork
      Small candle
      Penny
      Large eraser
      Pencil-tip eraser
      Raisin
      Button
   Food coloring

Bible Lesson

This Old Testament story is of special interest because it is often unfamiliar. It involves a miracle, mentioned only once in the Bible, by which God solved a workman's problem. Certain Israelites had gone to the Jordan River to settle. They were cutting wood for shelters when a minor accident occurred. An axhead came loose, flew through the air, and landed in the river. The workman was distressed over losing a borrowed tool, and he asked for help. Elisha located the spot where the metal piece had sunk, and tossed in a stick. Miraculously, the heavy axhead floated to the surface and was retrieved by the workman.

This rarely mentioned miracle shows God's complete power over nature, even in the smallest details. In truth, of course, no miracle is small. Each is a temporary reversal of the fundamental physical laws of nature. This axhead miracle answered the simple plea of help from an unnamed workman. It also encouraged Elisha and the others, and showed God's great glory.

Science Demonstration

This activity can be set up ahead of time or done with a small group. It explores liquids and objects of different densities. The idea is to help visualize the floating axhead story.

Slowly pour the liquids one at a time into the glass jar, perhaps over a spoon so they do not mix. The narrower the jar, the better. Pour the liquids in the order listed—most dense first and least dense last:

> Syrup or molasses
> Dishwashing liquid
> Water
> Vegetable oil
> Rubbing alcohol

When poured gently, the liquids should remain separate in distinct layers. Keep the amounts in proportion to nearly fill the container. Avoid getting the sticky syrup on the sides of the container.

Now introduce several small objects into the mixture. Gently place the objects on the surface and observe them. Certain items will float at a particular layer, while others will sink. Each object seeks its own resting place depending on its own density or heaviness. The final product is an interesting sight with the distinct liquids and suspended objects. For visual effect, add food coloring to the water before pouring it into the jar, and also use small objects that are colorful.

Explain to the group that the iron axhead that floated in water is an entirely different case that cannot be duplicated. Our liquids and objects are obeying scientific laws; the axhead obeyed God's direct command.

A clear container shows the colorful separation of liquids with different densities.

Science Explanation

Floating or sinking depends on the densities of materials. Density can be measured in grams per cubic centimeter (g/cm^3). Density takes into account an object's weight and also its size. The following table compares densities for several common materials.

Material	Density (g/cm^3)
Cork	0.24
Wood	0.3–0.6
Rubbing alcohol	0.87
Vegetable oil	0.91
Water	1.0
Dishwashing liquid	1.03
Syrup	1.37
Penny	9.0
Liquid mercury	13.6
Gold	19.3

Water density is assigned the value of one by the definition of the gram and cubic centimeter. Objects with a smaller density than one will float in water; more dense objects will sink.

3

Swirling Clouds

Theme: God controls the weather.

Bible Verse: *He brings the clouds to punish men, or to water his earth and show his love* (Job 37:13).

Materials Needed:
Clear drinking glasses
Water
Ink or food coloring

Bible Lesson

Weather is more commonly talked about than any other topic. The weather itself and the forecasters who bravely try to predict it are also the targets of many complaints. Job 37 gives a clear description of the many ingredients that can make up our daily weather: thunder and lightning (vv. 1–5), rain and snow (vv. 6–8), and wind and clouds (vv. 9–12). Verse 13 gives some basic reasons why God sends storms. For example, they may bring correction, as in the time of Noah. Storms may also bring needed moisture to the land. Lightning replenishes the soil with nitrogen so that crops can be produced. God's love is constantly shown as the earth is cared for and refreshed by the variety in the weather.

Job himself was no stranger to storms. A firestorm had burned up his sheep and servants (Job 1:16). Then a mighty wind suddenly killed all ten of his children (Job 1:19). Even then Job honored the Lord with these words:

> The Lord gave and the Lord has
> taken away;
> may the name of the Lord be
> praised (Job 1:21).

Job realized that God controls all the details of nature, including the weather. Perhaps we are too quick to complain about the heat, cold, or storms. God surely has his reasons for the weather, either rain or shine.

Science Demonstration

Participants will observe the unusual mixing of two liquids. Completely fill the drinking glasses with water, then let the water settle and become still for at least one minute. Several people can observe each glass. Gently place 2–3 drops of ink or food coloring on the top surface of the water. The dye is slightly heavier than water and will slowly sink. As the dye settles, it should form a small ring within the water. This ring will in turn separate into still smaller rings, and so on. Place more dye on the water's surface to repeat the intriguing process.

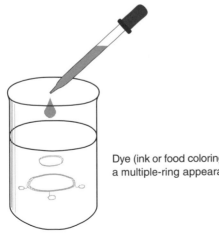

Dye (ink or food coloring) settling in water develops a multiple-ring appearance.

The unusual behavior of the moving dye illustrates the complex motion and mixing of air masses in the sky. Such atmospheric mixing does not form simple rings as observed here. Instead there are a large number of complex interactions continually occurring in the air.

The rings and turbulence observed within the glass of water are not completely understood by scientists. It is no wonder that weather forecasters are not always successful in their daily predictions. Only the Lord knows completely the details of tomorrow's weather.

Science Explanation

The sinking dye illustrates Bernoulli's principle (1738). This principle states that the pressure of a fluid decreases with increased velocity of the fluid. As the ring of dye settles in the water, the outer portion slows down slightly. This causes a slow rotation of the entire ring. Turning speed is greater within the dye ring, so the inside pressure is smaller and the ring holds together. Similar pressure differences may lead to the stability of tornadoes and hurricanes.

Instabilities within the sinking ring of dye soon lead to breakup, followed by several smaller rings. This process continues indefinitely until ended by the bottom of the glass or dilution of the dye. The observed motion of the dye is a combination of streamlined and turbulent fluid flow. This process has not yet been exactly duplicated by computer models. Complex fluid motions are some of the remaining unsolved mysteries of motion.

4

Keeping in Balance

Theme: God provides stability in a changing world.

Bible Verse: *I have set the* LORD *always before me. Because he is at my right hand, I will not be shaken* (Ps. 16:8).

Materials Needed:
Yardstick or broom
Long pencils or rulers for participants

Bible Lesson

Psalm 16 describes the confidence David experienced in his life. He faced many severe problems, yet still wrote this wonderful testimony. With the Lord at his side, David could not be moved or shaken. This means there was not the slightest danger of losing his position in Christ. Nor could he ever be disappointed with his decision to follow the Lord. David had tied his life to a secure refuge that would not fail. In this turbulent world we too can enjoy confidence in the Lord as David did. The promise of our key verse, Psalm 16:8, is repeated by Peter in Acts 2:25.

Science Demonstration

Demonstrate a technique for balancing objects in an unusual manner by holding the broom or yardstick horizontally for all to see. Rest it upon your 2 index fingers. Begin with the fingers widely separated for easy support of the stick. Now comes the interesting part: Slowly slide your 2 fingers inward toward each other. It is okay if 1 finger slides more than the other. When the fingers meet, the stick should remain horizontal and perfectly balanced. This balance point is at the center of the yardstick, and somewhat off center for the broom. Your fingers will automatically seek this position, also called the object's center of gravity.

Participants can easily repeat this balancing act with pencils or rulers. Have them support the item on their index fingers. The initial position of the fingers is not important. Then have them slide their fingers inward—the balance point is automatically found.

Now lock in the lesson idea. Stress that the Lord can keep our lives in balance. We all face daily pressures, temptations, and disappointments. These things can quickly throw us off balance and interfere with our Christian walk. But here is the good news: Christ can bring our lives back into balance. His power helped David and is still available today. Confidence in the Lord automatically provides us with a balance point in our lives.

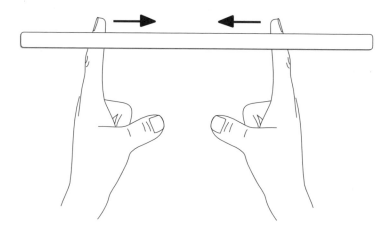

A stick of any length has a balance point, located by moving both fingers inward until they touch.

Science Explanation

Every object has a center-of-gravity position. This activity locates the balance point by sliding one's fingers inward while supporting the object. With a broom or ruler, the finger closer to the balance point supports most of the weight. This results in more friction and less ability to slide; the other finger slides instead. When both fingers are supporting equal weight, either they will both slide or they will alternate in motion. It is always the finger with less friction that slides. The differences are automatically sorted out by friction until the fingers meet at the center of gravity.

5

Blue Skies and Red Sunsets

Theme: God's colorful artwork fills the skies.

Bible Verse: *The heavens declare the glory of God; the skies proclaim the work of his hands* (Ps. 19:1).

Materials Needed:
Overhead projector
Large clear drinking glass or bowl
Drops of milk or dry milk powder

Bible Lesson

We are surrounded by the beauties of God's creation. On each new day it is easy to take many details for granted, including the clouds, blue skies, and breezes. Psalm 19 reminds us that God's creative work is everywhere, including the skies above. Day after day the sky shows its glorious colors: bright blue by day, red and orange hues at sunrise and sunset. On the moon, in contrast, there is no air and therefore no sky color. The lunar skies are continually black, both night and day.

In nature studies there needn't be any separation of science from the Bible. These two sources of knowledge work together and reinforce each other. For example, science explains the technical formation of sky colors, while Scripture explains their purpose. This purpose is to show God's glory and planning in the details of creation. It is God who has filled the earth with objects that are pleasant to our sight (Gen. 2:9). Even cameras cannot fully capture the artwork of God.

Science Demonstration

This demonstration is suitable for large groups. Participants might be asked to call out the colors they can presently see around them in window views, pictures on the wall, plants, people, pets—anything within sight. Stress that God gives these colors for our enjoyment.

The white light from the overhead projector can be partially separated into its colors. Place the clear container filled with water on the projector screen. Use caution to avoid spills whenever electricity and water are close together. Light from the projector should pass freely through the water to a screen or wall.

Now drop a generous pinch of the milk powder or several liquid milk drops into the water. Experiment ahead of time to find the proper amount. If the powder is slow to dissolve, stir it a bit. The tiny milk particles will act to separate the colors of white light. The blue color of the light is readily absorbed by the water, turning the water a blue-gray shade. This is similar to the blue sky formed when sunlight passes through the air. While observing the water, also watch the screen. It now shows the white light

Small particles of milk in water will separate light into its component colors.

minus its blue component, giving a brown-orange color. This is somewhat similar to the color of the sun and sky at sunrise or sunset. For smaller groups, the same effect can also be seen by shining a flashlight through a clear glass of water and adding the powder. Of course, the colors of indoor experiments cannot compare with the brilliant colors of the actual sun and sky.

Science Explanation

Blue skies and red sunsets arise from the scattering of sunlight. The process was first explained by British scientists Lord Rayleigh and John Tyndall in the late 1800s. The sun's light waves are absorbed by air molecules, then emitted again a moment later. The blue color, with a shorter wavelength than red, is more readily scattered across the sky. When the sun is low on the horizon at morning or evening, its light passes through additional air molecules and the red color now begins to scatter. Thus the bright orange-red sun colors are often seen at sunrise or sunset.

The complicated process by which air molecules scatter sunlight is not fully understood by scientists. However, this display of God's artwork in the sky can be enjoyed by all.

6

Amplifying Sound

Theme: God gifted us with an impressive and complex hearing system.

Bible Verse: *I praise you because I am fearfully and wonderfully made; your works are wonderful, I know that full well* (Ps. 139:14).

Materials Needed:
Sheets of paper
Tape
Straight pins
Old records if available
Fine-grain sandpaper

Bible Lesson

David was deeply impressed by the creation of life, as each of us should be. In our day, however, ideas contrary to creation abound, such as evolutionary origin and slow development through random mutations. David's testimony is a refreshing and timely contrast to such false ideas.

As just one example of creative design, consider our sense of hearing. Our ears allow us to enjoy birds and musical instruments, voices and songs. Hearing also protects us by warning of approaching danger.

The assumed evolution of the ear has not been explained in detail. Somehow our animal ancestors are said to have developed open canals beneath their skin, along with cells sensitive to sound vibrations. But consider the complex sequence of vibrations which must work together perfectly when one hears a sound. The sequence of sound vibrations moves through each of these objects in turn:

> Violin string
> Air molecules
> Outer eardrum
> Hammer, anvil, stirrup (the three smallest bones in our bodies)
> Inner eardrum
> Fluid within the ear's cochlea
> Hair follicles lining the cochlea
> Electrons within nerves at the base of the follicles
> The brain circuitry itself

When the vibrating electric signal finally reaches the brain, we hear beautiful music. All this happens in a split second, and with vibrations of hundreds or thousands of cycles per second.

How could such a complex system ever evolve slowly over time, and by chance? All the details of the ear must be present and working together for hearing to exist; the ear simply could not develop haphazardly or slowly. Similar examples of God's intricate design can be seen throughout our bodies and the entire creation. Evolutionary alternatives to David's testimony are neither convincing nor scientifically satisfying.

Science Demonstration

This demonstration explores the definition of sound as a vibration. A simple sound amplifier can be made with a sheet of paper and a straight pin. Roll the paper into a cone and tape it. An opening is not necessary at the tip; uneven paper at the flared end does not matter. Now reach inside and push the pin through the narrow end so the pin point protrudes outward to the side (not through the tip).

Hold the cone and pull the pin across an object; it will vibrate and the paper megaphone should amplify the sound. Also try rubbing the pin across cloth, sandpaper, or any other rough surface. A static sound will result as the pin vibrates unevenly.

Of more interest, the pin can bring out sounds stored in the grooves of an old record. Ideally the record should be spinning on a turntable. If a turntable is not available, one can also turn a record by placing a pencil through the center hole and spinning it. The process will not produce quality music, but the vibrating pin will produce small portions of the recorded sounds. Use an old record that is not valuable, since the pin will scratch its surface.

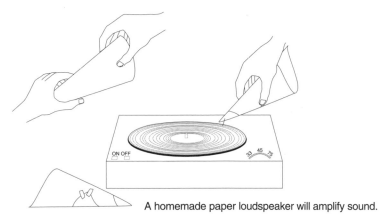

A homemade paper loudspeaker will amplify sound.

Science Explanation

Sound can be defined as a vibration, whether caused by a violin string, a drum, or a person's vocal chords. In this experiment the pin vibrates rapidly by passing over a rough surface. The paper cone attached to the pin also vibrates. The greater size of the cone then causes nearby air molecules to vibrate. This air pressure disturbance finally reaches our eardrums. The cone is somewhat similar to an audio speaker within a radio, television, or CD player.

7

No Air to Breathe

Theme: God's gift of salvation, not our works, opens the way to heaven for us.

Bible Verse: *There is a way that seems right to a man, but in the end it leads to death* (Prov. 14:12).

Materials Needed:
Empty aquarium or large bowl
Baking soda
Vinegar
Candle and match

Bible Lesson

Early on the morning of August 21, 1986, the people living near Lake Nios in Cameroon, West Africa, went about their chores. Cattle grazed on the hillside while children played games. Suddenly a vast cloud of invisible gas bubbled up from the lake bottom like an enormous fountain and spread outward across the land. The carbon dioxide gas had no taste or smell, but it was deadly. Wherever it flowed, animals and entire families quickly suffocated. In just minutes, 1,750 people and many thousands of cattle were killed without warning. The air, which appeared to be normal and healthy, had become poisonous. Scientists do not understand why the lake underwent this tragic sudden change, nor can they predict when it may happen again.

The Scripture verse reminds us that we can be sadly mistaken about the important things in life. For example, people have many different ideas about salvation and gaining a home in heaven:

Some get baptized and attend church without fail.

Some hope their good deeds will outweigh the bad.

Some give gifts to church or charity to "pay their way."

Some repeat special words or phrases thousands of times.

None of these methods is sufficient! As hard as one may try, it is simply impossible to *earn* a ticket to heaven. Motives and deeds may seem good enough, but by themselves they lead to failure. The morning air seemed good enough to the poor people around Lake Nios, but it actually was deadly.

The Bible makes it clear that salvation is a gift given to those who place their faith in Christ (Eph. 2:8–9). Good deeds are fine, but are not sufficient to gain eternal life. Christ has already paid the price for us—take him at his word!

Science Demonstration

This demonstration produces invisible carbon dioxide in the aquarium. Add baking soda and vinegar to the tank, about 1/2 cup of each. The mixture will bubble and foam at the bottom. Carbon dioxide is heavier than air and will remain in the tank for several minutes.

Now light a candle in front of the group. Slowly lower it into the tank and the fire should quickly go out; carbon dioxide will not support a flame. If this doesn't work well increase the amounts of baking soda and vinegar to make more carbon dioxide. Explain to the group that the tank looks clear and breathable, but its contents are actually suffocating to the candle. Likewise, as our verse clearly states, some people's choices on the path to heaven may look good, but actually cause spiritual suffocation.

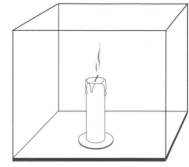

An aquarium containing vinegar mixed with baking soda shows the suffocating properties of carbon dioxide gas.

Science Explanation

Baking soda is sodium bicarbonate, $NaHCO_3$; vinegar is acetic acid, $HC_2H_3O_2$. Their reaction together can be written as:

$$NaHCO_3 + HC_2H_3O_2 \rightarrow CO_2 + H_2O + NaC_2H_3O_2$$

The bubbling gas is carbon dioxide, CO_2; this gas is heavier than most other gases in the air. Here is a comparison table of the four most common gases in our atmosphere:

Gas	Relative Weight	Percent Abundance in Air
Argon, Ar	10	.93
Nitrogen, N_2	14	78.0
Oxygen, O_2	32	21.0
Carbon Dioxide, CO_2	38	.03

The carbon dioxide will not remain permanently in the container because gases slowly diffuse or spread outward into the surrounding air. The small amount of carbon dioxide produced is not dangerous. After all, we exhale carbon dioxide continually.

For further exploration, blow soap bubbles and let them fall into the aquarium. They contain some nitrogen and should float on the invisible carbon dioxide layer, suspended midway in the tank. As an alternative to vinegar and baking soda, Alka Seltzer and water can also be used to release carbon dioxide.

8

Dancing Raisins

Theme: Seek the Lord's direction.

Bible Verse: *The plans of the diligent lead to profit as surely as haste leads to poverty* (Prov. 21:5).

Materials Needed:
   One dozen raisins
   Clear drinking glass
   Large bottle of clear soft drink (soda pop)

Bible Lesson

We live in a world of rapid movement. Airports and highways are crowded; information surges through electronic networks. We often feel the stress from this busy lifestyle. We must make quick decisions, then we suffer the consequences if things go wrong.

In the Book of Proverbs King Solomon cautions us regarding hasty decisions. Whenever possible, we should exercise the ability God has given us to think through to the results of our actions. It takes extra effort to consider the consequences, but this effort is very worthwhile. Many potential problems can be avoided in this way. For example, major purchases should be preceded by considering their impact on our budget. We must also remember that a quality purchase is often wiser than a substandard bargain.

Notice that Solomon's proverb refers to material gain. This is certainly not the chief goal in life, but profit rather than poverty can enable us to help others and also to avoid financial tensions. Not all problems or opportunities that come our way can be anticipated. However, many can, and people who plan ahead will enjoy a calmer life as a result.

Dancing raisins rise and fall in a solution containing carbon dioxide gas.

Science Demonstration

Years ago this activity commonly involved dropping mothballs into water. As the mothballs dissolve, carbon dioxide bubbles form on their surfaces and float them to the top. There the bubbles break loose and the mothballs sink back to the bottom. The restless up and down motion of the mothballs humorously illustrates our modern lifestyles.

The demonstration can be done more simply by dropping raisins into a glass of clear soda pop. The raisins gather carbon dioxide at the bottom, float to the top, then drop downward again. This works best if one uses fresh, dark raisins and room-temperature soda. Raisins are not essential; peanuts, buttons, uncooked spaghetti, or other small objects will also gather bubbles and float. While watching the "dancing raisins," ask the participants if their schedules sometimes are similar: much running around with little real progress being made. Ask for suggestions on how we can prevent hasty mistakes, unproductive errands, and wasted time. The list might include:

Asking God for direction through prayer.

Seeking counsel from others.

Combining several errands into one trip.

Taking adequate time for reflection before making major decisions.

Science Explanation

Soda pop has considerable carbon dioxide, CO_2, dissolved within it. This results in dilute carbonic acid, which gives it the familiar tangy taste. At warmer temperatures the soft drink can hold less gas so it bubbles upward. You have probably seen the result of a rapid loss of carbon dioxide when a soft drink container is vigorously shaken before opening. As an alternative to soda pop, Alka Seltzer and water also release carbon dioxide.

The raisins or other small objects have a density just slightly greater than water. If small bubbles of CO_2 attach to them, they are buoyed upward to the surface. They will remain there until the bubbles separate, then they drop downward again.

9

Whiter than Snow

Theme: God's forgiveness is complete.

Bible Verse: *Though your sins are like scarlet, they shall be as white as snow; though they are red as crimson, they shall be like wool* (Isa. 1:18).

Materials Needed:
Large jar with cover
Strips of colored construction paper
Liquid bleach

Bible Lesson

Christopher was a mess when he finally arrived home from school. Earlier it had looked like a good day for bicycling. By afternoon, however, a light rain was falling. The bike ride home started out okay, just a few raindrops, which felt good on his skin. Soon, however, Christopher was having difficulty dodging the puddles. A wide streak of brown mud from the rear wheel began forming up the back of his white jacket and even in his hair. As many others have found out, it is hazardous to ride a bicycle in the rain!

Finally Christopher was within sight of home, with the mud now dribbling down his forehead. He made quite a sight as he stood dripping inside the kitchen door. The opposite of a white snowman, Christopher now was covered with dirt. Instead of being upset, Mom couldn't help but laugh at the sight and Christopher did the same. Into the shower he went while his dirty clothes were taken directly to the laundry room. Very soon Christopher was clean again and wearing dry clothes. Even his jacket was white again.

Christopher thanked his mom for rescuing him. Together they remembered their breakfast devotion. It was about the Lord washing away sins and making lives as white as snow in his sight. In fact, the Bible said that God no longer *remembered* the sins of his children (Jer. 31:34, Heb. 8:12). "Okay, Mom," Christopher said, "how soon will you forget this muddy afternoon?"

Science Demonstration

Carefully pour about $\frac{1}{2}$ to 1 inch of liquid bleach, into a large, wide-mouth jar . Stand the colored strips of paper inside the jar, partially submerged. Put the cover on the jar to avoid fumes.

It should take just minutes to bleach the strips to a white color. If some color remains, you can stress that only God does a perfect job of removing stains. Have some of the original paper available nearby to show the contrast in colors. The comparison is quite impressive, and will help lock in the "white-as-snow" concept of forgiveness.

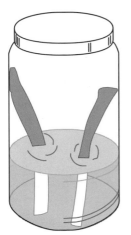

Strips of construction paper are bleached white.

Science Explanation

There are several forms of bleach, one of the most common being a solution of sodium chlorite, $NaClO_2$. The bleaching activity is largely due to chlorine dioxide, ClO_2. The chlorine oxidizes many colored substances to colorless compounds. Large amounts of chlorine are used commercially in bleaching wood pulp for paper and also in making cotton cloth. Typical sources of chlorine are brine wells, salt mines, and ocean water.

10

A Blind Spot

Theme: New life in Christ opens our spiritual eyes.

Bible Verse: *Then will the eyes of the blind be opened and the ears of the deaf unstopped* (Isa. 35:5).

Materials Needed:
Paper
Pencils or pens

Bible Lesson

Isaiah chapter 35 is a beautiful picture of Israel's future from the prophet Isaiah's vantage point around 700 B.C. The good news is best enjoyed when compared with the dire judgment of chapter 34. The eyesight and hearing described in our key verse picture the gift of salvation. Knowing God, our eyes and ears are opened to things we simply couldn't see before:

> God's love for us
> The value of God's Word
> Answers to prayer
> God's leading in our life
> The glories of creation

The verse also had a literal fulfillment when Christ walked among mankind fifty generations ago. At that time he physically healed the eyes and ears of many needy people. Surely Christ had Isaiah 35 in mind when he sent a message of hope to John the Baptist (Luke 7:19–23). What a Savior we have, one who can heal eye and ear problems, both physical and spiritual.

This activity reminds us of the complexity of our eyes. We all have a blind spot, though, and can miss seeing things. Likewise, the person who does not know God is blind to the greatest gifts in life. New life in Christ opens our eyes to these gifts from above.

Science Demonstration

Participants need a piece of paper and a pen or pencil. Each person is asked to draw an X and O about $\frac{1}{2}$ inch high and as dark as possible on the paper side by side, with X on the left. The letters should ideally be spaced about $2\frac{1}{2}$ inches apart—the same as the distance between the eyes.

Now hold the paper at arm's length. Look at the X with your right eye, while closing or covering the left eye. The O should still be seen far off to the right side. Very slowly bring the paper closer to your eye. At about 8 inches distance, you should notice that the O completely disappears from the page. The paper is now located at your blind spot. Nearer or farther away, the O will reappear. Any marks on the paper will suffice; the X and O are simply convenient symbols to see.

As a paper with two letters on it is moved closer to your eye, you notice a blind spot when one letter disappears.

Try reversing the experiment, covering the right eye and looking at the O with the left eye while moving the paper. The same effect will result, this time with the X disappearing from view.

Science Explanation

Light passes through the eye's cornea and lens, focusing upon the retina on the back surface of the eyeball. This retina is filled with millions of light sensors called rods and cones. There is one spot on the retina, however, where the optic nerve connects the eye to the brain. Sensors are lacking in this small region. When light focuses on this blind spot, an image cannot be seen. Most often this is not noticeable since one eye compensates for the other. When one eye is covered, however, as in this demonstration, the blind spot becomes apparent. The optic nerve connection, or blind spot, is actually located off center on the retina, so visual problems are usually avoided, even with just one eye. The Creator thought of everything!

11

Solving a Puzzle

,

Theme: Nature's laws show God's faithfulness.

Bible Verse: *But God made the earth by his power; he founded the world by his wisdom and stretched out the heavens by his understanding* (Jer. 10:12).

Materials Needed:
   Bowls of water
   Paper cups
   Small weights such as coins, marbles, or stones
   Masking tape

Bible Lesson

What would happen if the sun stopped shining today? Our earth would quickly grow very cold and dark. And what would happen if the force of gravity suddenly switched off? We would slip off the earth and float into space along with all the animals, rocks, and seas. The earth would also disintegrate into fragments with gravity no longer holding it together. But thankfully, the sun and the force of gravity continue to operate day after day.

Thousands of experiments are performed every week in research laboratories and classrooms across the land. Identical experiments always give the same results. If an experiment doesn't work as it should, then some condition or variable has been changed from before. Every laboratory result verifies that nature is predictable. This predictability is what makes scientific research possible, and it is rooted directly in our Scripture reference. God has created a universe which is based on wise laws of operation. Solar energy does not radically change, nor does the gravity force become erratic.

Science by itself provides no assurance that identical experiments will always give the same results. In the theory of a random, evolutionary universe, gravity might operate on Tuesday but not on Thursday. Whether we realize it or not, it is God's careful maintenance of nature that makes it predictable and makes our daily lives possible.

Science Demonstration

This activity works well with smaller groups of 2–4 people. It involves close observation to solve a puzzle. Begin by posing a difficult question:

Suppose you are floating in a pool on an air mattress. You are also holding a laptop personal computer. Suddenly you drop the computer, which sinks to the bottom along with all your work! Now the question: When the computer sinks, will the water level of the pool rise, fall, or remain unchanged?

The answer is not obvious and the listeners may not agree. You might have them vote on the 3 choices to show the difference of opinion. Stress that nature is consistent; there *is* a correct answer to the puzzle.

Now have small groups find the correct answer by experimenting. In a large container of water, perhaps a kitchen bowl, float a smaller vessel such as a paper cup or cupcake wrapper. A heavy object should be placed in the smaller vessel—a stone, marbles, or perhaps several coins. Mark the water level at the edge of the bowl with a small piece of masking tape. Now the floating weight, like the computer, should be dropped overboard. Note carefully how the water level of the bowl changes—

it should *drop* slightly. This result is quite unexpected; it shows how we may easily talk ourselves into the wrong conclusion. However, nature always gives the correct result as it has been programmed to do by its Maker.

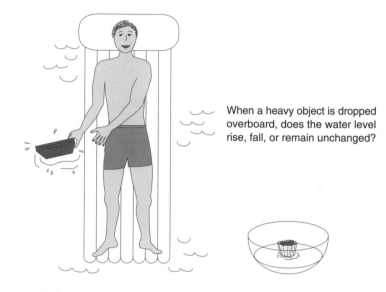

When a heavy object is dropped overboard, does the water level rise, fall, or remain unchanged?

Science Explanation

Here is the rule for all floating objects: A floating object's submerged portion displaces an amount of water equal to the object's total weight. If a toy boat weighs one pound, cargo and all, it will push out of the way or displace one pound of water as it floats. This rule is called Archimedes' principle and has been known for two thousand years.

Suppose the computer in the puzzle weighs 18 pounds and has an airtight volume of 100 cubic inches. This weight is 5 times heavier than the equal volume of 100 cubic inches of water. While floating on the air mattress the computer will displace 500 cubic inches of water, or 18 pounds of water. When completely submerged, however, the computer will displace only 100 cubic inches of water. On the bottom of the pool the computer is no longer buoyed up or floating, so its weight is no longer a factor. It only displaces equal volume.

Thus the water level will drop slightly, although not enough to notice in a large pool.

Here are some related situations to ponder:

If a boat or ship sinks in a confined area, the water level will likewise drop somewhat.

A ship floats higher in salt water than in fresh, because salt water is slightly heavier or more dense.

Suppose the swimmer in the puzzle was holding a large block of ice instead of a computer. If the block slid into the pool or else melted completely, the water level would remain exactly the same. Likewise, when ice melts in a beverage glass the liquid level is unchanged.

12

Wonderful Water

Theme: God's showers of blessing include his creative design of water.

Bible Verse: *I will bless them and the places surrounding my hill. I will send down showers in season; there will be showers of blessing* (Ezek. 34:26).

Materials Needed:
Two glass thermometers
Paper towel
Water
Electric fan

Bible Lesson

Ezekiel 34:25–31 describes a future time when God will heal the land and care for his people. This will include showers of blessing, the title of a well-known hymn written by Daniel Whittle a century ago,

> There shall be showers of blessing,
> This is the promise of love;
> There shall be seasons refreshing,
> Sent from the Savior above.

Rain showers provide many benefits for the earth: cleansing of dust and chemicals from the air, watering of plants, recharging of ground water aquifers, and filling of ponds and reservoirs. Without rain, the earth would soon become a difficult place for life to exist. In our exploration of space, we have found no other planet with rain showers, or any liquid water at all. There is no place like home! The passage in Ezekiel reminds us that God's blessings are like refreshing rain. In fact, his blessings are much more precious than rain because they never end.

Science Demonstration

This demonstration shows that the evaporation of water is a cooling process. You will need 2 glass thermometers, the kind with small bulbs at the bottom. They should be easy to read, and identical or at least similar.

Thoroughly wet a small piece of paper towel and wrap it loosely around the bottom bulb of 1 thermometer. Hold the thermometers side by side and show the group that both give the same degree reading. Now turn on the fan and place both thermometers in the breeze. The plain thermometer will not change its reading substantially. The "wet bulb" thermometer with the paper towel at the base should drop in temperature, perhaps 6–10 degrees, within 2–3 minutes.

This experiment shows how our bodies are cooled by the evaporation of perspiration. The process removes many heat *calories* from our skin, regulating our body temperature. Without

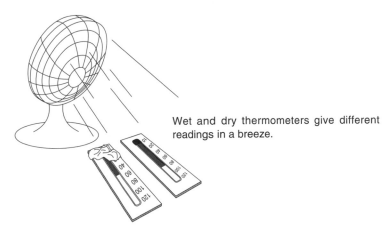

Wet and dry thermometers give different readings in a breeze.

this ability, hot weather would bring much greater danger of sunstroke or heat exhaustion. When the humidity is high, skin evaporation is hindered and one feels uncomfortable. Humidity is actually a greater factor than the temperature in determining our comfort level.

Science Explanation

Evaporation is a wonderfully complex process. Water consists of vibrating, moving molecules. Collisions between these molecules within the liquid can cause some of them to leave the surface and move into the air. They become water vapor or humidity.

The average speed of water molecules is a measure of the water temperature. When the faster molecules escape, the remaining water temperature therefore drops. This is exactly what we observe with the thermometers. The breeze causes faster water molecules to escape from the wet paper towel, cooling it and also cooling the thermometer. Meanwhile, the dry thermometer changes little. A weather forecaster compares wet and dry thermometers in a similar way with a device called a psychrometer. The humidity of the air can be accurately measured in this way. Low humidity is indicated by a large difference between the wet and dry bulb readings.

In dry climates, swamp coolers operate on this principle. They evaporate water and circulate the resulting cool air around the room. Also, you may notice this cooling effect when alcohol is rubbed on your skin by a nurse before an injection. The alcohol evaporates very quickly, removing calories of heat from your skin in the process.

If we could only see the trillions of water molecules within a drop of water! They are rapidly moving about in a blur, with some ricocheting into the surrounding air. There is fascinating activity on the small, invisible scale of atoms and molecules.

13

Harmless Fire

Theme: God protects his children.

Bible Verse: *They saw that the fire had not harmed their bodies, nor was a hair of their heads singed; their robes were not scorched, and there was no smell of fire on them* (Dan. 3:27).

Materials Needed:
Small hand towel or cloth
Metal tongs
Container for mixing liquids
Salt
Water
Matches or lighter
Bottle of rubbing alcohol (isopropyl alcohol)

Bible Lesson

Daniel enjoyed a long life of service to his Lord. Along with the lions' den experience, the fiery furnace story stands out in the Book of Daniel. Daniel's friends Shadrach, Meshach, and Abednego refused to worship a gold image that King Nebuchadnezzar had made. Daniel was about 30 years old at this time, and he and his three friends faithfully worshipped only the true God of their Jewish background.

The selfish king became furious and had the three men tied up and thrown into a blazing fire. However, the Lord was present and protected them. In the intense fire the king could see the men walking about accompanied by a protecting angel. Their ropes were unbound in the flames and they were perfectly safe. When the men came out of the furnace they were untouched by fire or even smoke. God had supernaturally protected his children as a great sign of his power and love. King Nebuchadnezzar understood this message and honored the Lord and his faithful servants.

Science Demonstration

In the container mix equal parts of water and rubbing alcohol, about 1/2 cup of each. Also dissolve a generous pinch of salt. Just before the demonstration, soak the cloth briefly in the liquid mixture. Ring it out slightly to avoid drips and remove any alcohol from your hands.

Tell the group that just as Daniel's friends were protected from the fire, likewise the cloth will not burn. Lift the wet cloth upward with the tongs and hold a lighted match or lighter at the bottom. The flame will slowly envelope the cloth. The salt adds an orange color to the fire; without salt the flame is light blue and somewhat difficult to see. It also helps to momentarily turn off the lights. After the flammable alcohol has burned off, the fire should go out. If not, hold the towel securely and snuff out the flame with a quick jerk. The water prevents the still damp cloth from igniting.

After the demonstration, explain that Shadrach, Meshach, and Abednego experienced a *miracle* while we simply performed an experiment. Some may want to feel the wet cloth; remind them that the three men had no such water shield available. Feel free to explain why the cloth does not burn; this is not meant to be a magic trick. In a different setting this activity can also be performed with a soaked dollar bill instead of cloth. Then it becomes a humorous example of "burning money."

Whenever there is the slightest fire hazard, you should know the location of a nearby fire extinguisher. It is also a wise precaution to have a damp newspaper spread over your working surface.

A cloth can be made to burn without
being scorched.

Science Explanation

Isopropyl alcohol, C_3H_7OH, vapor readily burns with a blue flame; the chemical is not explosive. The flame warms up the cloth but cannot ignite it as long as water is present in the cloth's fibers. The combustion reaction is

$$2C_3H_7OH + 9O_2 \rightarrow 6CO_2 + 8H_2O + \text{Heat}$$

The fiery furnace may have been heated like a blacksmith's hearth. This would make use of high-temperature fuel and a bellows system for air flow. Such a fire would roar loudly and could nearly melt the brick walls of the furnace. In this way a temperature of 1000°F is attainable, hot enough to burn the unfortunate soldiers who were nearby (Dan. 3:22).

14

Walking Together

Theme: Friendship with Christ means walking in his ways.

Bible Verse: *Do two walk together unless they have agreed to do so?* (Amos 3:3).

Materials Needed:
Fresh egg
Hard-boiled egg

Bible Lesson

It is a delight to take a relaxing walk with a friend. Ideas and encouragement can be easily shared in this setting. Walking with someone is beneficial for both mind and body. Sometimes, however, a friendship is sadly broken by disagreement. Then the friends can no longer walk together in peace, and both suffer as a result. Conflicts quickly remove the joy of walking and talking.

Our key verse refers to Israel's broken relationship with God. After leaving Egypt in the exodus, the Jewish people soon turned away from the Lord. The Israelites still expected God's benefits and protection, but they no longer worshipped him. The prophet Amos told the Israelites that they could not expect God's presence and protection unless they returned to him. Over and over again in history, Israel turned away from the only one who could bless them.

The answer to the question of Amos 3:3 is a clear *No*. Both parties must be in agreement for harmony to result. God had not changed, but Israel had instead fallen away from fellowship. Amos was giving the people a wake-up call to their need for repentance.

Make sure that your friendship with others remains strong and positive. If there has been a breakdown in communication, make the first move toward restoration. Even more importantly, we must consider our relationship with God. Are we walking with him? If not, it is we ourselves who need to change.

Science Demonstration

"Walking together" can be illustrated with 2 eggs, one hard-boiled and one fresh. Show the group how easily the hard-boiled egg spins on a table. With a large audience this can be done on an overhead projector. Once spinning, the egg can be quickly stopped by placing your finger on it.

The fresh egg represents disagreeing friends who cannot walk together. Try spinning the fresh egg exactly like the hard-boiled one. There is now a problem: The harder you try to spin a fresh egg, the less easily it turns. It resists the spinning motion. You can explain that the liquid materials inside the fresh egg are pulling against each other. Once the fresh egg is turning slowly, place your finger on top to stop the motion, then quickly let go. The fresh egg will start spinning again and continue turning slowly by itself.

Fresh

A hard-boiled egg spins and stops more easily than a fresh egg.

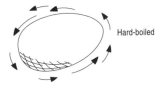

Hard-boiled

Agreement with a friend is shown by the boiled egg, which readily spins and stops just as expected. It is entirely dependable. Disagreement is shown by the fresh egg; it behaves erratically and does not do what is expected. Let's be more like the boiled egg and behave like dependable friends.

Science Explanation

The behavior of the 2 eggs follows from Isaac Newton's first law of motion, also called the law of *inertia*. This word means "lazy" or "sluggish." The rule states that objects at rest or in motion remain that way, unless they experience a changing force.

The boiled egg is solid; it spins easily and also stops quickly. The fresh egg, however, contains a yolk floating in the liquid egg white. In this egg, the yolk's inertia causes it to lag behind and resist the turning motion. When this egg finally is turning, stopping it does not completely halt the movement of the yolk within. The yolk bumps against the inside of the shell and causes the egg to turn again slowly. The parts of the fresh egg pull against each other and prevent a smooth turning motion.

15

Rocks That Fizz

Theme: God outlasts the mountains.

Bible Verse: *He stood, and shook the earth; he looked, and made the nations tremble. The ancient mountains crumbled and the age-old hills collapsed. His ways are eternal* (Hab. 3:6).

Materials Needed:
  Vinegar
  Clear glass container
  Any combination of
    chalk
    small seashells
    eggshells
    limestone or cement fragments

Bible Lesson

Mountains are usually considered to be ancient and permanent features. Their majesty is one of the greatest sights in all of creation. However, Habakkuk 3:6 gives a totally different perspective: Compared with the Lord, even the mountains are insignificant and temporary.

The Book of Habakkuk describes God's holiness and also his patience with evil. Our key verse pictures the end times at the

conclusion of this present world system. The mountains are not
exempt; they will quickly crumble. Revelation 16:20 further
states that someday the mountains and islands will disappear. It
is important to remember that all physical things on earth and in
the sky above are temporary. Someday, perhaps soon, the Lord
will return and make new heavens and a new earth. Only what
is done for God has lasting value.

Science Demonstration

This activity shows how hard, permanent objects can be dissolved away. Neither mountains nor rocks last forever. Pour 1
cup or more of vinegar into a clear glass container. The stronger
the vinegar, the better. Vinegar is usually diluted to 4–10 percent acidity, according to the label. It may help to let an open
glass of vinegar set for several days. Water will evaporate away,
leaving behind the stronger vinegar solution.

Several of the listed objects can be dropped into the vinegar.
The vinegar is a weak acid and will cause the objects to bubble
and slowly dissolve. It may take some minutes or hours for
some objects to noticeably dissolve. The listed objects, including limestone, are all composed of the mineral calcite. A small
piece of limestone from outdoors is especially impressive to use
since we usually think of rocks as indestructible. Limestone is
quite common in most areas, and is sometimes used as crushed

Various common materials containing calcite
will fizz and slowly dissolve in vinegar.

stone for driveways. If chalk is placed in the vinegar, small pieces will soon break off, and finally the chalk totally disappears. Comment to the observers that no physical objects on this earth are permanent.

Science Explanation

The dissolving process is a speeded-up version of acid rain. Precipitation is somewhat acidic and reacts chemically with surfaces: Car paint tarnishes, plant leaves become unhealthy, and tombstones slowly become unreadable. Vinegar is a diluted form of acetic acid, $HC_2H_3O_2$. The mineral calcite has the formula $CaCO_3$. When these chemicals come in contact, the gas that bubbles off is carbon dioxide, CO_2:

$$CaCO_3 + 2HC_2H_3O_2 \rightarrow H_2O + Ca^{++} + 2C_2H_3O_2^- + CO_2$$

This reaction is regularly used by geologists as a test for the mineral calcite in unknown rock samples.

16

A Smothered Candle

Theme: The gospel must be shared.

Bible Verse: *Neither do people light a lamp and put it under a bowl. Instead they put it on its stand, and it gives light to everyone in the house* (Matt. 5:15).

Materials Needed:
  Votive candle
  Matches
  Large clear bottle or glass
  Shallow bowl
  Water
  Food coloring

Bible Lesson

In our early Sunday school years we sing

> This little light of mine,
> I'm going to let it shine . . .
> Hide it under a bushel, no!

This light pictures our new life in Christ. If we truly comprehend what he has done for us, we will be compelled to share Christ with others. How can such exciting, life-changing news be kept under cover? The Scripture term for bowl (bushel in the KJV) is a dry measure of volume, about 1 peck in Bible times, or $\frac{1}{4}$ the size of a modern bushel basket.

Matthew 5:16 goes on to acknowledge the good deeds which result from a Christ-centered life. The verse teaches that hiding one's Christian light either under a bushel or behind a closed door is selfish. After all, any praise which others give for our good deeds belongs to God, not to us.

Science Demonstration

Place the lighted candle in the shallow container. It should be partially submerged in water. The depth of water is unimportant, as long as the glass will easily fit over the candle and down into the water. The candle is now burning brightly. Next, put the glass in place over the candle and down into the water. Several interesting things will happen quickly. The candle will continue burning for a few seconds. It will also heat the air inside the glass, causing large gas bubbles to leave the bottom of the glass. Then the candle will go out as it exhausts its oxygen supply. The air remaining inside the glass then cools and contracts, pulling water back up into the glass. The rising water level is more easily seen if a small amount of food coloring has been added to the water.

The candle burns fine as long as it is in the open. However, when sealed up inside the glass without oxygen, the flame cannot continue burning. Likewise, the Christian life is not designed to be sealed up and kept a secret. The Good News is meant to be shared with others.

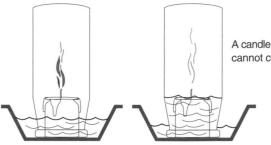

A candle trapped under a glass cannot continue burning.

Science Explanation

This experiment is often explained incorrectly. The burning candle is said to use up all the oxygen, resulting in a vacuum which pulls the water upward into the glass. This is not true! The oxygen gas is converted to an equal amount of carbon dioxide gas, not a vacuum. As the candle goes out from lack of oxygen, it is the cooling, contracting air which then causes a partial vacuum inside the glass. A simple combustion reaction can be written for the candle involving carbon, C, oxygen, O_2, and the resulting carbon dioxide, CO_2:

$$C + O_2 \rightarrow CO_2$$

When the air initially expands by heating, its volume change is proportional to the temperature increase. If the air inside the glass doubles in temperature, then a glassful of air escapes in the initial bubbling process. When the candle is extinguished, the remaining air likewise cools and contracts. It is quite surprising how high the water level rises inside the glass.

17

Sink or Swim

Theme: God knows our hearts.

Bible Verse: *All the nations will be gathered before him, and he will separate the people one from another as a shepherd separates the sheep from the goats* (Matt. 25:32).

Materials Needed:
Aquarium or deep, clear bowl
Water
Assorted unopened soda pop cans, diet and regular

Bible Lesson

Matthew writes of a future time when those who know the Lord will be selected from all the people of the earth. Scripture is very clear that this day of judgment will come. For the believer this is a great encouragement: Someday justice will prevail on the earth. For the unbeliever this promise should be a great motivation to turn to God.

It is impossible for us to judge the motives and hearts of others. We see only the outside of a person, but God looks within the heart and mind. He certainly knows us better than we know ourselves. His judgment is 100 percent accurate and fair.

Science Demonstration

This activity compares the densities of several kinds of canned soft drinks. The unopened cans are dropped one at a time into the water-filled aquarium. A little showmanship is in order—have the audience guess which cans will float or sink as you drop them in.

A pattern will quickly be noticed: Cans of diet soda float while the others sink. There may be some rare exceptions if a particular can is not completely filled with liquid. The demonstration is fun and probably would make a good soft drink commercial! It shows how readily the cans can be separated into categories, using the property of density or weight, which is not obvious from the outside appearance.

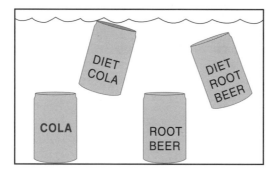

Cans of diet soft drink float in water while the sugared variety sinks to the bottom.

Science Explanation

Most diet sodas are sweetened with NutraSweet, also called aspartame. This artificial sweetener is lighter in weight than the sugar in ordinary soda. Soda cans are not completely filled with liquid; a small amount of carbon dioxide gas is noticeable by the splashing sound when an unopened can is shaken. In diet soda, the gas and the aspartame result in a product that is less dense than the aquarium water and the can therefore floats. Meanwhile, the sugared soda is heavier and sinks to the bottom of the aquarium. In a random sample of several cans of soft drink, I found that the sugared variety averaged 5 percent heavier than the diet drink.

18

Creating a Picture

Theme: People, made in the image of their Creator, are a special part of creation.

Bible Verse: *But at the beginning of creation God "made them male and female"* (Mark 10:6).

Materials Needed:
   Poster board (any color)
   Ruler
   Scissors
   Pencils

Bible Lesson

There is a popular assumption today in science that we somehow evolved from an animal. We are said to be an advanced form of animal, but not really any different from all other forms of life on the earth. Our key verse makes clear the error of this thinking. From the beginning, mankind has been a unique part of creation. Not only are we separate from animals, but we have been given charge over them (Gen. 1:26).

Many differences exist between people and animals. We have complex languages, a sense of history, and accumulated knowledge through our generations. Another area of our uniqueness is artistic creativity. We have been blessed with minds which can produce an unending variety of beautiful music and works of art. Animals do not have this ability. A robin has a particular song that is beautiful but largely unchanging. Its nest is intricate but is the same design season after season. The robin is programmed to instinctively do robinlike activities. It simply is not capable of experimenting with new songs or new types of nests. So it has ever been for robins since creation, as well as for other kinds of animals. Beautiful spiderwebs or flowers further show God's handiwork, not that of the animals and plants themselves. Human creativity truly sets us apart, further showing our special creation in God's image. After all, he is the great artist and creator, and he stamped his image upon us.

Science Demonstration

Participants will experiment with a tangram puzzle. They can either cut out their own puzzle or be provided with the pieces. The figure shows how to cut a square into 7 pieces as shown in the illustration. Begin with a square of cardboard with 6-inch sides. Mark off 2 diagonal lines, and divide 1 of them into 4 equal segments. Then draw the other lines as shown before cutting out the pieces.

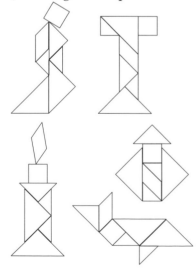

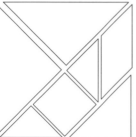

The tangram is an ancient puzzle that takes many forms. Shown are the puzzle pieces and several pictures.

Now it is time to be creative. Challenge participants to create biblical pictures using all 7 pieces such as a cross, church, star, candle, camel, or whale. Various letters and designs can also be formed. There are thousands of possible pictures. The participants can try to guess each other's creative designs. Remind them that this simple activity illustrates our unique difference from the animal world. Evolution clearly is wrong; we are a special creation. All forms of life have a common Creator, not a common evolutionary ancestor.

Science Explanation

The tangram is an ancient Chinese game that stimulates thinking. During the 1800s, this puzzle was very popular throughout the United States and the world. An 1844 British children's magazine complained about young people who wasted hours on the Chinese puzzle to little purpose! Elaborate ivory carvings of the puzzle are now valuable antiques.

Puzzle pieces include a square, rhomboid, and 5 triangles. The goal is to use all 7 pieces to make a design or figure. Entire books have been written to show the possible patterns. I have not yet been able to construct a symmetric cross; can you? The figure shows some typical results.

19

Not Enough Pull

Theme: God is able to save us.

Bible Verse: *Jesus looked at [the disciples] and said, "With man this is impossible, but not with God; all things are possible with God"* (Mark 10:27).

Materials Needed:
Two plungers with long handles

Bible Lesson

Jesus had just told his disciples that it was difficult for a rich man to enter the kingdom of God. In fact, it would be easier for a camel to pass through the eye of a needle. The disciples were astonished at this apparent impossibility. Mark records Jesus' reply to the disciples' confusion.

In truth it is impossible for anyone to enter the kingdom of God on his or her own merit. No matter how good we are, we all fall far short of God's perfection. No matter how much money we have or give away, we cannot buy a ticket into heaven. Now the good news: With God all things are possible, including our salvation. What we cannot do, God freely does for us by his love and grace.

Science Demonstration

This activity involves a tug of war. Push 2 plungers firmly together. The challenge is to pull them apart again. Perhaps 2 people can grasp each plunger. Have them sit on the floor so no unexpected falls occur. Participants will quickly find that it is nearly impossible to separate the plungers by pulling outward. It seems to be an impossible task, like the kind of predicament that perplexed the Lord's disciples.

To separate the plungers, simply turn them so the handles are at right angles to each other. Air should seep between the rubber seals and allow them to easily fall apart. What formerly seemed impossible is actually quite simple. Make clear to the audience that this is a very limited analogy to Mark 10:27. When we know the secret we can separate the plungers. However, gaining salvation by ourselves truly is impossible, with no simple shortcut. Our eternal life is possible only through Christ's sacrifice for us.

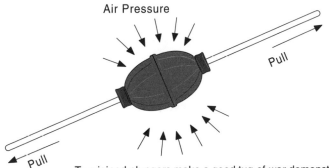

Two joined plungers make a good tug-of-war demonstration.

Science Explanation

A famous demonstration was performed in 1654 in Magdeburg, Germany. Scientist Otto von Guericke brought 16 horses and 2 large copper bowls before the emperor. The metal bowls, each about 2 feet in diameter, were placed snugly together with a leather fitting. The inside air was then removed with a pump. Eight horses were harnessed to each copper hemisphere in an effort to pull them apart; they barely succeeded. This dramatic demonstration showed the surprising effect of air pressure. With no air or pressure inside the copper hemispheres, the weight of the outside air pushed the spheres together with many tons of force.

When 2 plungers are pushed together, the inside air is expelled. A plunger that is 5 inches in diameter has an outside surface area of about 40 square inches. Each square inch of the outside surface experiences a force from the air pressure of about 15 pounds. Thus the plungers are held together by an invisible force of several hundred pounds. It is no wonder that the tug of war does not easily succeed. When the plungers are turned at right angles, the inside vacuum is broken as outside air is admitted. The unbalanced outside pressure difference then disappears.

20

Walking on Eggshells

Theme: God tenderly cares for us.

Bible Verse: *Are not five sparrows sold for two pennies? Yet not one of them is forgotten by God* (Luke 12:6).

Materials Needed:
Several eggshells
Masking tape
Scissors
Several books

Bible Lesson

Who cares about sparrows? There are billions of these common birds. The answer is that God made them and he also cares for them. Sparrows in Scripture refer to any small bird of the finch family; they are still found throughout Israel. Each sparrow contributes its chirps, beauty, and nonstop activity to our world. Sparrows spend most of their waking hours in search of food. They don't live long; the record for a sparrow in captivity is ten years. God has given all types of birds instinctive knowledge about nest building, egg care, and feeding their young.

God values his children far above sparrows. In fact, he knows the very number of hairs on our heads (Luke 12:7). Just as God provides for the animal world, so he also provides for us. Christians are not on their own in this world; God watches out for us in many ways that we do not realize.

Science Demonstration

This activity shows how well the Creator cares for baby birds within their eggshells. Obtain 3 or 4 eggshell halves by cracking fresh eggs. Run masking tape around the broken edges, then trim the edges smooth and even with scissors. The tape will prevent the shells from cracking; it can be left on or removed after trimming.

Now place the eggshells, all roughly the same height, on a table with open ends down. These small egg domes provide "legs" for a book that is gently laid upon them. Add additional books to make a stack on the eggshells. Carefully add even more until 1 of the shells finally collapses. The books should add up to an impressive amount of weight. You might have a strong volunteer pick up the stack of books to demonstrate the effort needed. When perfectly balanced, a single eggshell has been shown to support the entire weight of a person!

The eggshell provides a strong home for a baby bird. The shell easily withstands the weather and the weight of the sitting mother. The baby emerges by breaking the shell from the inside out. This is a much easier task than breaking an egg from the outside.

Eggshells will support a heavy load.

Science Explanation

The dome form of an eggshell is one of the strongest shapes possible. The thin shell is made of calcium carbonate, $CaCO_3$, which isn't very strong in itself. However, when the book weight is applied to the top of the dome, the force is transferred along the shell surface to the base. This force tends to compress the eggshell and is strongly resisted. The dome shape is often used as a roof in large stadiums and arenas where supporting columns are not practical.

Here are two other ways to show the strength of an eggshell. If you hold a fresh egg in your palm, it is nearly impossible to crush the egg by squeezing the ends together. Try this over the kitchen sink! Be careful since the edge of an eggshell can cut. You can also safely toss a fresh egg upward as high as possible above a grassy lawn. The strength of the eggshell and the cushion of grass will almost always prevent the egg from breaking when it lands.

21

A Downhill Race

Theme: Be faithful to God.

Bible Verse: *Do you not know that in a race all the runners run, but only one gets the prize? Run in such a way as to get the prize* (1 Cor. 9:24).

Materials Needed:

Board such as a table leaf

Hollow cylinders (paper towel roll, empty soup can)

Solid cylinders (dowel, thread spool, unopened can of food)

Solid balls (golf, softball, rubber ball, marble)

Hollow balls (tennis, hollow rubber ball, ping-pong ball)

Bible Lesson

The background of our key verse is the great athletic contests that were held during New Testament times. In Corinth the Isthmian Games took place, a festival of athletic and musical competition. The sports included wrestling, discus throwing, and running. This tradition continues today as the Olympic Games.

Most people enjoy competitive sports, either as participants or observers. In a race there can be only one first-place winner. And to win, the runner must prepare well, as successful athletes in your audience will readily testify. The prize may only be a ribbon or trophy, but this token is overshadowed by the great honor of finishing first. In Paul's day, the typical prize was a small pine wreath placed on the head of the winner.

Paul points out the great effort and sacrifice necessary to win a competitive prize. Yet far greater is the honor to be gained by being faithful to God. One can tell from the passage that Paul enjoyed sports, but he loved serving the Lord even more. How do we compare with Paul today?

Science Demonstration

Everyone likes a race, and you can provide one. The race down a sloping surface will be between four different objects: solid and hollow balls, and solid and hollow cylinders. The group might like to vote on which object will most likely win the downhill race. If the objects are similar in size and weight, the results are pre-determined by physical laws of motion.

It may be difficult to have all four objects roll down the board at once. In this case the objects can be released two at a time, with the winner going on to the next round. To start a race fairly, hold the objects at the top, perhaps behind a yard stick. Then quickly raise the stick without pushing the spheres or cylinders. The race ends at the bottom of the slanted track.

A downhill race between different objects has predictable results.

Science Explanation

Various objects falling through the air have identical motion if air resistance is small. Thus a dropped stone, a book, or a pen all will hit the floor closely together. A ramp race involves the rolling of objects, a more complicated process. Here the *shape* of the objects becomes important. Rolling motion is resisted by

76 Science and the Bible

an object's moment of inertia, called I. This I takes into account the size and distribution of matter within the object itself. Here are some moment of inertia values for several items, where R is the object's radius and M is the object's mass or heaviness:

Object	I: Moment of Inertia
Solid sphere	$2/5 \, MR^2$
Solid cylinder or disk	$1/2 \, MR^2$
Hollow sphere	$2/3 \, MR^2$
Hollow cylinder or ring	MR^2

A solid sphere has the smallest I value, so it will roll the fastest. A hollow cylinder or ring has a large I value and therefore generally lags behind the other shapes. The material that makes up a cylinder or ring is farther away from the rotation axis, and this slows the rolling motion. In contrast, the sphere has more of its mass close to the rotation axis and therefore it turns easily.

22

Members of the Family

Theme: Each member of the church family is important.

Bible Verse: *Now you are the body of Christ, and each one of you is a part of it* (1 Cor. 12:27).

Materials Needed:

Several paper coffee filters

Scissors

Washable dark-colored felt-tip pens (black, brown, green, etc.)

Clear glasses with small amounts of water

Bible Lesson

Your body is made up of many parts: 206 different bones, 100,000 miles of blood vessels, and biological complexity beyond imagination. Every component works together for the benefit of your body. If even one small part fails to perform, however, pain or sickness may quickly result.

The body of Christ (1 Cor. 12:27) is descriptive of the local church. A congregation is made up of people with various gifts, abilities, and interests. Taken together they all contribute to a healthy, functioning church family. No person whom God brings into the local church is more or less important than the others. If one person is missing, the church body is incomplete.

The mark left by a felt-tip pen results from several component colors. Each of these colors is chosen and combined by the manufacturer for the desired result. If any component color is missing, the result will not be the same. The function of each internal color may not be obvious, but it is very real. Members of the local church family are like the colors within the pen. Each is different; each is also essential for the planned result.

Science Demonstration

Cut several strips 1 inch wide from the coffee filters, each about 6 inches long. Give 1 or more strips to each participant. Now distribute washable felt-tip pens, overhead transparency pens for example. Have each person draw a dark line across the strip 1 inch from an end. Strips can be marked with different colors, but black, brown, or green give the most interesting results. Suspend the paper strip in a glass containing 1 inch of water. The ink line should be about $\frac{1}{2}$ inch above the water level. Make sure the line is not submerged. Fold the strip over the top edge of the glass to hold it in place. More than 1 strip can be placed in the same glass as long as they do not touch.

Water immediately will begin soaking into the paper and moving upward. In crossing the ink line the water will dissolve color pigments and carry them upward at different rates. Within a few minutes, the colorful components of the ink will be displayed on the upper portions of the paper strip. Compare the strips to see the variety of dyes within the ink. The strips later can be dried and kept as unusual bookmarks.

Inks show a variety of internal color dyes.

Science Explanation

This procedure is called paper chromatography. It is often used to separate pigments that are present in objects such as plant leaves. (In this case place a leaf on the filter paper and roll a coin back and forth over the leaf to leave a green stain.) Capillary action within the absorbent paper draws water upward until it reaches the top of the glass. It is important to use washable pens, or the color separation will not readily occur. Transparency pens work well, and also children's marking pens. Pigments or dyes within the ink are dissolved by the water at different rates. The easily dissolved dyes are carried upward by the water. Less-soluble dyes are delayed and remain near the bottom of the paper strip. In this way, a gradual separation of pigments occurs. Some felt-tip colors may have only one pigment. The black, brown, and green, however, are made with a variety of colors. Black pens from different manufacturers may also give different results.

Crime laboratories sometimes use chromatography to separate the components of substances. For example, the particular ink used in a ransom note may be clearly identified in this way, somewhat like a fingerprint.

23

Looking in the Mirror

Theme: In time we will understand God's plan.

Bible Verse: *Now we see but a poor reflection as in a mirror; then we shall see face to face. Now I know in part; then I shall know fully, even as I am fully known* (1 Cor. 13:12).

Materials Needed:

Paper

Pen or pencil

Square or rectangular mirror (at least 6 inches long)

Bible Lesson

The city of Corinth was famous in the apostle Paul's time for its production of mirrors. These were polished bronze surfaces, much inferior to modern glass mirrors. The readers of Paul's letter would readily understand the meaning of a poor reflection, compared to one's actual appearance. An unclear mirror image provides an excellent comparison to our present and future understanding of God's plan.

Today we wonder about many things in life:

Why don't we get our own way?

Why is there sickness and pain?

When will the Lord return?

Someday the answers to such questions will be made crystal clear to us. Meanwhile we can have confidence that God knows what is best for us. God looks down from above and sees all things from beginning to end.

Science Demonstration

This activity points out the unusual reflections in a small mirror. Participants are asked to explain what they observe. Various words are printed on paper in capital letters. The words are then reflected in a mirror.

An interesting word pair to begin with is HYMN BOOK. Write this in large letters. Now line up the mirror just above the word, perpendicular to the paper, so you can see both the writing and the reflection. You will find that the word HYMN is upside down while BOOK is unchanged. Why does this happen? Some participants will solve the puzzle quickly; others will not understand the result. Many other words and pictures also have interesting reflections. These examples are especially interesting:

CARBON DIOXIDE	BIKE	RAWHIDE
KITCHEN COOK	BOX	LIVE OX
HIDE OR SEEK		

You might also have participants write their names and check the reflections. In the end, be sure everyone understands why the reflected words appear as they do. Explain that what was at first a mystery has now become clear. Likewise, God's ways may presently be poorly understood. In time, however, all our questions will be answered.

Some words have strange reflections in a mirror.

Science Explanation

Words reflected in the mirror are turned upside down. However, certain letters are shaped so that they are unchanged when inverted. They are symmetric in the vertical direction. These special capital letters are limited to

B, C, D, E, H, I, K, O, X

If lowercase letters are used, the list is reduced to just three:

c, o, x

The mirror does not do anything unusual to the words. It is the letters themselves that cause the unusual results.

24

Bursting with New Life

Theme: Believers must share the gospel.

Bible Verse: *Therefore, if anyone is in Christ, he is a new creation; the old has gone, the new has come!* (2 Cor. 5:17).

Materials Needed:

Handful of hard, dried seeds (peas, beans, corn, or lima bean seeds work well)

Sand

Water

Small clear container that can be sealed, perhaps a glass jar or plastic pill bottle

Bible Lesson

As growing seeds soak up water, they come alive and can no longer be confined. These seeds illustrate the new believer. When new life is found in Christ, exciting changes will occur. The person can no longer "keep the lid on." Instead, he or she will want to tell others about their new direction. Over time, many positive changes should also be evident in their life.

Once the gift of salvation has been received, who would want to go back to a life that is empty? Likewise, a growing seed cannot be forced back into its original hard shell. Instead, the seed grows and eventually reproduces itself many times over.

Science Demonstration

This experiment requires a day or two for completion. Mix seeds and sand in equal amounts. Pour this mixture into a jar, shaking the jar to fill it completely. Now wet the sand thoroughly. Screw the lid on tightly; it need not be airtight. As the seeds absorb water and swell, the expansion will pop the cap from a pill bottle, or crack a glass jar. If glass is used, put the container on a cookie sheet to prevent a spill. For a single Bible lesson, the before and after results can be prepared ahead of time to be shown together. If time permits, a container can be loaded up during a lesson and put aside for future inspection. Sometimes seeds swell quickly, and may even pop the container during the lesson itself.

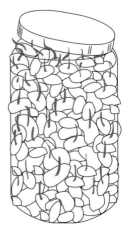

Swelling seeds are able to break almost any container.

Science Explanation

Seeds can be stored in a dry, dormant form for many years or even centuries. When moisture is present, however, the growth process begins immediately. The seed coat has a small opening, often on an indented side, that admits water. The inner embryo or germ of the seed readily absorbs this water, swelling in the process and cracking its outer shell. In this way the seed begins to produce a root and stem.

The pressure exerted by a growing seed or plant is tremendous. Perhaps you have seen a plant gradually overturn a rock or raise a slab of concrete. Plant growth depends strongly on water movement through small capillary tubes in the plant. It is the changing internal water pressure in the tubes that folds leaves at night and opens blossoms by day. This complex hydraulic action has been operating ever since plants were made on the third day of the creation week.

The swelling of moist seeds was responsible for the sinking of a large supply ship during World War II. A vessel carrying sacks of dried beans was slightly damaged by a torpedo. The ship continued on its way, but the cargo of beans became soaked and started to swell. Eventually, the expansion of the beans split open the hull of the ship, causing it to sink. The vessel survived the torpedo, but not the growth of its cargo of sprouting seeds!

25

A Shield

Theme: Stop Satan in his tracks.

Bible Verse: *Put on the full armor of God so that you can take your stand against the devil's schemes* (Eph. 6:11).

Materials Needed:
Small battery-operated radio with an internal antenna
Various wrappings (paper bag, cloth, leather)
Sheet of aluminum foil

Bible Lesson

It is natural to protect ourselves from danger. Wearing a seat belt is one such wise precaution. However, there are certain dangers that demand special attention. Ephesians 6 describes the devil and his dark powers. Satan's attacks have destroyed many political leaders, pastors, and even entire families. Simply put, Satan seeks to ruin your life and your Christian testimony. He is our enemy, but God provides special weapons to combat this evil. The weapons listed in Ephesians 6 include

Truth and righteousness (v. 14)
The gospel of peace (v. 15)
Faith, salvation, and the word of God (vv. 16–17)
Prayer (v. 18)

One might think that these weapons are invisible and therefore not effective. However, the truth is just the opposite. Exercise these gifts and meditate on them; Satan then will be powerless to intervene.

Science Demonstration

Turn on the radio to music that everyone can hear. You will want to try this ahead of time to find suitable music. You will be demonstrating what can stop the incoming music signal. The radio will continue playing inside a paper bag, wrapped in a cloth, or put in a purse. You can even cover the radio with your body, and the signal will pass completely through you to the antenna. Clearly it is difficult to stop a radio signal. Remind the listeners of the devil's schemes, which can penetrate our own defenses and lead to failure.

Now wrap the radio completely in the sheet of aluminum foil; one layer should be sufficient. The layer of metal will absorb the incoming signal and quiet the radio. Although the foil is thinner than the other wrappings, it quickly stops the music. In a similar manner God's defenses for us—the invisible, spiritual weapons listed in Ephesians—are entirely sufficient to protect us from the devil's schemes.

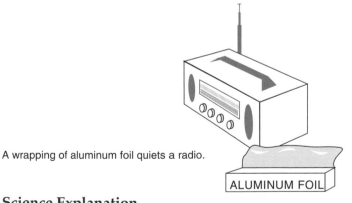

A wrapping of aluminum foil quiets a radio.

Science Explanation

Radio signals are also called electromagnetic waves. They are an invisible form of light which travels at the fantastic speed

of 186,000 miles per second in air. These waves easily penetrate the walls of a house, allowing radios to operate. Metal,
however, completely stops the radio waves. The wave energy is
dissipated as electrons within the metal are made to vibrate;
the waves then cannot reach the radio antenna. This is why an
external radio antenna is required to hear music inside a metal-
lic automobile.

26

A Bubble of Water

Theme: God holds the universe together.

Bible Verse: *[Christ] is before all things, and in him all things hold together* (Col. 1:17).

Materials Needed:
Pennies
Eyedroppers
Water
Paper towels

Bible Lesson

Scientists have learned much about the forces of nature. It is the gravity force that keeps us on the ground, and the electric force which holds atoms together in all objects. We can write down formulas for these forces, but our understanding remains limited. What really is gravity, or electric charge? We do not know; these are simply terms for describing what we observe.

Colossians 1:17 tells us that Christ has established the laws of gravity and electricity. And he maintains them day by day. Consider the alternative: If the Lord turned his back on the universe for just one moment, instant chaos would result. Water, the land, the moon—all would disintegrate. Christ remains very much in charge of his universe, for our daily benefit.

Science Demonstration

Each participant is given a penny, eyedropper, small container of water, and a table or flat surface to work on. The object is to see how many drops of water can be placed on the face of the penny before water overflows the side. Instead of eyedroppers, any kind of straw or squeeze bottle that releases single drops will work. The surface tension or stickiness of water results in a rounded bead of water on the penny. As water drops are carefully added, the growing bubble or "skin" of water will rise and wobble. The water drops will hold together in an impressive bubble. Eventually, gravity overcomes the water's surface tension and a small spill occurs. Have paper towels nearby for the cleanup. If time permits, have participants count the drops as applied to compete with each other for the highest number.

Surface tension allows many drops of water to remain on a penny.

Science Explanation

Water has one of the highest surface tensions of any common material. In the following comparative list, only mercury has a greater surface tension.

Liquid	Relative Surface Tension
Ethyl alcohol	.29
Ammonia	.31
Soapy water	.33
Sulfuric acid	.73
Blood	.80
Water	1.0
Mercury	6.5

This high surface tension of water has many practical benefits:

Water climbs up the narrow capillary tubes of plants and
trees to water the upper leaves.
Watery fluids cling to our bone joints and also our eyes
for constant lubrication.
Surface tension causes raindrop formation.
Soil remains moist as water drops cling to each other and
to soil particles.

Water molecules are drawn toward each other because of an
attractive electrical force. Slightly positive hydrogen atoms in
one water molecule are attracted to negatively charged oxygen
atoms in surrounding molecules. This forms a hydrogen bond
that is responsible for many of water's special properties.

For further study, add a drop of soap solution to a penny
that is covered with water. Soap reduces surface tension, causing
the water to quickly spill off the coin. This soap property helps
water droplets separate so they can move inside cloth fabric
during clothes washing. The water can then dissolve dirt within
the material fibers and carry it away.

27

Danger—Deep Water

Theme: Obey your parents.

Bible Verse: *Children, obey your parents in everything, for this pleases the Lord* (Col. 3:20).

Materials Needed:
Large clear glasses
Water
Pennies

Bible Lesson

Cari and her father stood at the edge of the swimming pool looking down into the water. They could clearly see the black lines painted on the bottom. The inviting water looked shallow enough for easy wading and Cari asked for permission. Dad cautioned her that water is often deeper than it looks, and therefore one must be very careful around pools. They stepped into the water together and Cari was surprised. The water was indeed deep and she tightly held on to her dad. The pool, which had looked so friendly a moment ago, was now a place of danger for her.

Cari's father further explained that many people have been fooled by the unexpected depth of water. Lifeguards are trained to watch for safety misjudgments by inexperienced swimmers.

In Cari's eyes the pool was shallow and safe. However, this was an incorrect assumption. She needed her dad's help to avoid the deep water. God has given us parents and other help-ful adults to protect us and care for us. Grown-ups have already experienced many of the hazards of life. Their parents once taught them about life's dangers. This valuable pattern of one generation helping the next pleases the Lord. It is *not* a sign of weakness to obey your parents; instead it is a sign of wisdom.

Science Demonstration

This activity shows why Cari was confused by the pool water's depth. Each person or small group is given a glass filled with water. A coin is dropped into the filled glass and then looked down upon from above. A second coin is placed on the table surface close to the glass and also observed from above. The submerged coin will appear to be somewhat elevated and will look closer to your eye than the dry coin. It is an interesting sight: The coins are obviously at the same level, table level, yet they look quite different.

The water in the glass appears shallower than it actually is, just as is true for any swimming pool. Water depth always acts this way, which is actually a mixed blessing. This effect makes diving somewhat safer because water is deeper than it appears; there is more room for underwater clearance. For a child step-ping into a pool, however, shallow-looking water that is actually deep can lead to an accident.

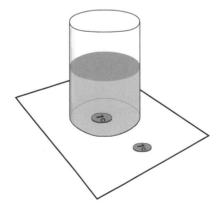

A penny looks magnified when it is submerged in water.

Science Explanation

The *apparent* depth of water is always less than the *actual* depth when you look down from above. This results from the slowdown of the speed of light in water. Light travels only 75 percent as fast in water as in air. Here is a comparison of several water depths:

Actual depth	Apparent depth
6 inches	4.5 inches
1 foot	9 inches
4 feet	3 feet
10 feet	7.5 feet

In each case the actual depth is multiplied by 0.75 to find the apparent water depth.

Apparent depth results in several other interesting illusions. You may have noticed some of these:

Your legs appear shorter or more stout when you stand in water.

Items underwater can be difficult to pick up. They are often not positioned where they appear to be.

A partially submerged oar or paddle often appears to be broken or bent.

A pencil or finger placed in a filled glass and observed from the side appears to be enlarged or magnified.

All these effects result from the slowdown and bending of light in water, also called light refraction.

28

Spreading Outward

Theme: Run from sin.

Bible Verse: *But you, man of God, flee from all this, and pursue righteousness, godliness, faith, love, endurance and gentleness* (1 Tim. 6:11).

Materials Needed:
  Bowl
  Water
  Pepper
  Liquid dish soap

Bible Lesson

There is a time to stay and fight, but there is also a time to *flee*. In 1 Timothy 6 several harmful practices are listed, including the teaching of false doctrines (v. 3), unhealthy interest in controversies (v. 4), and the love of money (v. 10). Whatever form it may take, the Christian should flee from sin. Like pepper floating on water, we need to stay as far away from temptation as possible.

In contrast, our key verse names the abundant good things we should pursue: righteousness, godliness, faith, love, endurance, and gentleness. These qualities will lead to fulfillment in this life and also the life to come.

Science Demonstration

Fill the bowl with water. Give the water a minute to settle and become still. Sprinkle some pepper on the water's surface; it will float like dust particles. Now gently place a drop of liquid dish soap in the center of the surface. (You can also touch a moist finger to a bar of soap, then dip your finger in the bowl.) The soap film should quickly spread out, carrying the pepper particles instantly to the outer edges of the bowl.

The pepper represents a believer, and the soap drop is an evil influence. (Some young children might already think that soap is bad!) The pepper immediately flees the soap, as a believer should flee sin.

If a large group is involved, this demonstration can be done in a clear, shallow tray of water on an overhead projector. The depth of water is not important. Other substances such as talcum powder can also be used in place of pepper. However, the dark color of pepper gives it a visual advantage.

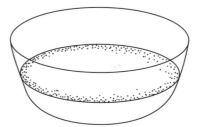

Floating pepper particles are pushed outward by the soap film.

Science Explanation

When the drop of soap is applied to water, it spreads out like a very thin pancake. The pepper is light enough to be pushed out of the way by the expanding soap film. Soap weakens the surface tension of water (see lesson 26) in the center of the bowl. The unaffected water molecules around the outside edge then pull the pepper specks together.

On a larger surface of water, soap will spread outward in a circle that may be several feet across. The layer becomes as thin as possible, the thickness of a single soap molecule. Benjamin

Franklin and other scientists first used this technique in the 1700s to estimate the size of individual molecules.

Some activity books recommend using a drop of cooking oil instead of soap. However, I find the soap works best. Within minutes the soap will completely dissolve into the water. This may sink the pepper particles as the soap further breaks down the water's surface tension. Before repeating the experiment, all traces of soap must be washed from the bowl.

29

Silly Putty

Theme: An unstable person is of two minds—
unsure whether or not to trust God.

Bible Verse: *He who doubts is like a wave of the sea,
blown and tossed by the wind. . . . he is a double-minded
man, unstable in all he does* (James 1:6, 8).

Materials Needed:
  Cornstarch
  Water
  Popsicle or stir sticks
  Tablespoon measure
  Coffee mugs
  Small plastic bags

Bible Lesson

James 1:5 invites the believer to ask God for wisdom and
understanding about daily decisions. There is one requirement
for this help, however. The request must be made with no
wavering or doubt (v. 6). A doubter is not sure whether God
hears him, or if God even understands his plight. Such a man is
double-minded; he attempts to divide his trust between God
and himself.

This unfortunate person can be humorously compared to Silly Putty. The strange material does not keep its shape; instead it always tends to flow downward. The putty has no strength; it can easily be twisted, bounced, or flattened. Silly Putty is unstable and cannot be trusted to maintain its shape. Likewise, the unstable person cannot be trusted as an example to follow because he lacks the balance of God's wisdom.

Science Demonstration

The participants will make their own "Silly Putty," an amusing rubbery substance. Have each participant follow this recipe:

Place about $\frac{1}{2}$ cup of cornstarch in each mug. Put newspaper under the mug to catch any spills. Now slowly add water, stirring with the popsicle stick. Add water until a gooey, fluidlike consistency results. If too much water is added, additional cornstarch will thicken the material. Fingers can also be used in mixing. You have now made your own form of Silly Putty, which can be pulled from the cup.

This interesting material can be stretched and shaped, but it will slowly spread out and flatten when left on its own, somewhat like thick syrup. Place a small object on the putty and watch it sink out of sight. When quickly pulled apart, the putty will break like plastic. If pressed against a newspaper the putty also may pick up some of the print.

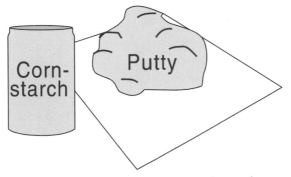

Homemade Silly Putty displays unusual properties.

Science Explanation

The putty is a suspension of cornstarch in water. This material has dual properties of both a solid and a liquid. It flows like a liquid, but can also be broken and pulled apart. It appears wet, but becomes powdery if rubbed between your fingers. This putty withstands the sudden shock of being hit, but it cannot support the weight of objects laid upon it. Other familiar non-Newtonian fluids, as they are called, are paint, ketchup, and commercial Silly Putty. Although this putty is nontoxic, participants should wash their hands afterward. If placed in a pocket or on furniture, the putty will slowly enter the fabric. In such cases it can be dissolved away with warm water. The putty can be stored in a closed plastic bag. After prolonged storage the putty may develop mold—discard it if this occurs.

Silly Putty originated in 1943, during World War II efforts to make synthetic rubber. James Wright, a Dow Corning engineer, first made Silly Putty. He put this new material away on the shelf, thinking it a poor substitute for rubber. Later, someone realized that the putty made a cute toy. Introduced on the Howdy Doody Show in 1957, Silly Putty quickly became a national fad. More recently the putty has been useful as a grip strengthener and also as an art medium.

30

Turning a Ship

Theme: The power of the tongue must be used wisely.

Bible Verse: *Or take ships as an example. Although they are so large and are driven by strong winds, they are steered by a very small rudder wherever the pilot wants to go. Likewise the tongue is a small part of the body, but it makes great boasts* (James 3:4–5).

Materials Needed:

Clear jar or drinking glass

Water

Cap from a ballpoint pen (bullet shape works well)

Small amount of clay

Large balloon or rubber glove

Rubber band

Bible Lesson

The Johnsons were on vacation and were aboard a large car ferry headed to an offshore island. This was ten-year-old Scott's first ride on a large boat and he enjoyed every detail. However, all the surrounding water was a bit frightening. The feeling was not helped when he saw another ferry in the distance, coming straight toward them. "I'm sure these ferries have made the trip hundreds of times," thought Scott. "But what if they should collide *today*, when we are on board?"

Scott's father saw him staring at the other ferry and realized Scott's concern. Dad asked Scott if he knew how a captain steered his boat. "Is it like a car's steering wheel?" guessed Scott. Dad then explained that steering a boat in water involves a rudder. It is like holding a paddle in the water to turn a canoe. A ship's rudder likewise will turn the boat to the left or right.

By now the other ferry was passing by at a safe distance. They could see the top portion of its rear rudder, which guided the boat's path. The rudder's small size was surprising on such a large ferry. Dad reminded Scott of James 3:4–5, where a ship rudder is compared with the tongue. Both are powerful steering agents. Words can steer people either in right or wrong directions. "Just as the two ferries passed safely," said his father, "let's be sure that our words are also safely used toward others."

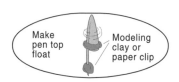

The position of the Cartesian diver can be easily controlled.

Science Demonstration

In this activity individuals or small groups will build Cartesian divers. This is a small object that rises or falls in water on command. Begin by adjusting the cap of a ballpoint pen so that it just floats in a glass of water. Tilt the cap underwater to let some air bubbles out. A small amount of clay or a paper clip can be pushed on the bottom of the cap to slightly weigh it down. This balancing step will take a few tries, so be patient.

When the pen cap is mostly submerged but just barely floating, fill the glass almost completely with water. Stretch a sec-
tion of rubber from a balloon or glove across the top of the glass
and secure it with a rubber band. Now push slightly downward
on the top and the pen cap should slowly sink to the bottom of
the glass. Release the pressure and the cap should rise. You can
make the cap bob up or down at will, or even keep it halfway
down in the glass.

The cap movement is an analogy with James 3:4–5, only with
a submarine instead of a surface ship. The sub is easily steered
upward or downward in the water by a soft touch on the top
balloon cover. Our control of the pen cap is a reminder of how
we must control our words since they can have a great impact
on others.

Science Explanation

The Cartesian diver was invented by the French scholar René
Descartes (1596–1650). Science activity books describe many
ways to build a diver. I have found the ballpoint pen cap to be
the simplest method. The diver rises and falls due to pressure
changes. Pushing on the top rubber membrane slightly increases
the pressure throughout the water. Whatever object is used to
make the diver, it must be open at its bottom. Increased pressure pushes water upward inside the diver, compressing the
air bubble inside. In this way the diver becomes heavier than
water and it sinks. If carefully balanced, a very slight pressure
change is sufficient to move the diver up or down.

Thanks for your interest in these object lessons. Hopefully they will increase your enjoyment of both Bible and science study. If you would like to see additional activities, please contact Baker Books or your Christian bookstore for another volume by the same author. The author also welcomes your comments on these activities.

Donald B. DeYoung is a scientist, author, and professor of physics and astronomy at Grace College, Winona Lake, Indiana. His other books, which also demonstrate the order and grandeur of creation, include *Astronomy & the Bible, Weather & the Bible,* and *Science & the Bible,* Volume 1.